CATAMARAN RACING

CATAMARAN RACING

Kim Furniss & Sarah Powell

Fernhurst Books

© Fernhurst Books 1993

First published in 1993 by
Fernhurst Books, 33 Grand Parade, Brighton, East Sussex BN2 2QA

Printed and bound in Great Britain

British Library Cataloguing in Publication Data
A catalogue record for this book is available from the British Library.

ISBN 0-906754-90-9

Acknowledgements

We would particularly like to thank the following people who contributed to this
book. The guys from Hobie Cat (UK) Ltd: Roger Tushingham, David Bangor-Jones,
Paul Pascoe, 1992 Hobie National Champion, and Mike Gething from Hobie Cat
(South West) who kindly loaned his Hobie 16 for the photo shoot. Performance
Sailcraft (Europe) Ltd, manufacturers of the Dart, for working so hard to provide an
excellent, well sponsored international racing circuit combined with a strict One-
design concept. Tim Davison of Fernhurst Books for being brave enough to ask us
to write the book and for his tremendous expertise and guidance throughout. And
last but not least our parents: Gordon and Rita Furniss who introduced Kim to
sailing by building his first boat in their sitting room; and Michael and Dawn Powell -
particularly Michael who instilled in us a dedication to win combined with a sense of
very fair play, and whose inspiration is sadly missed following his sudden death.
Thanks to them all.

                                                    Kim Furniss and Sarah Powell

Photographic credits

All photographs by Julia Claxton, with the exception of those supplied by the
following individuals and agencies:
Kos Picture Source Ltd: pages 39, 59, 69, 73, 78-9, 81, 89, 95, cover.
S. Toy: pages 6, 32, 33 (top), 35, 42, 43, 44, 48, 49, 57 (lower sequence), 58.
Yachting Photographics: pages 8-9, 34, 60, 64.
The publishers would particularly like to thank Dawn Powell for her hospitality
during the photo sessions.

Edited and designed by John Woodward
Artwork by PanTek, Maidstone
Cover design by Simon Balley
Printed and bound by Ebenezer Baylis & Son, Worcester

Contents

Introduction   6

Part One: Speed Sailing   9

Part Two: Race Tactics   59

Part Three: Preparing the Boat   85

Part Four: Tuning the Rig   89

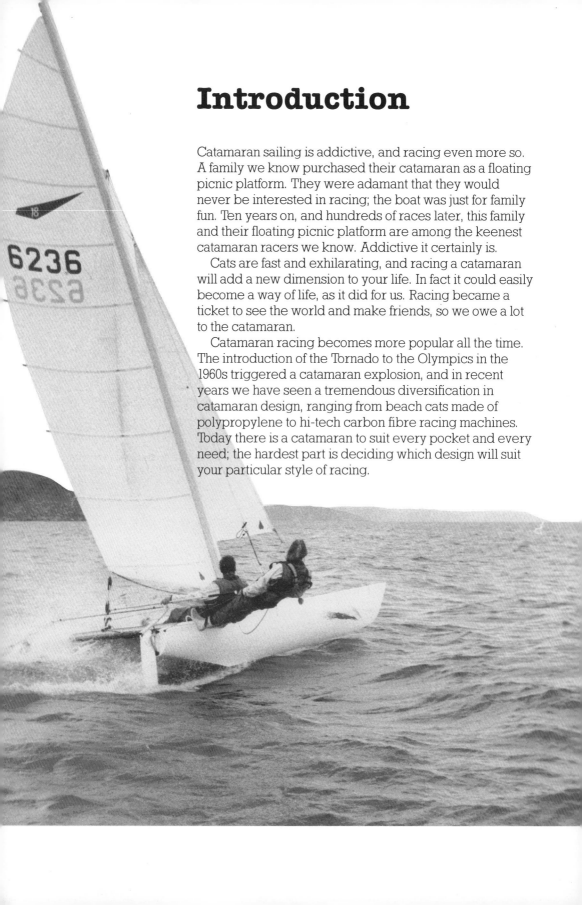

Introduction

Catamaran sailing is addictive, and racing even more so. A family we know purchased their catamaran as a floating picnic platform. They were adamant that they would never be interested in racing; the boat was just for family fun. Ten years on, and hundreds of races later, this family and their floating picnic platform are among the keenest catamaran racers we know. Addictive it certainly is.

Cats are fast and exhilarating, and racing a catamaran will add a new dimension to your life. In fact it could easily become a way of life, as it did for us. Racing became a ticket to see the world and make friends, so we owe a lot to the catamaran.

Catamaran racing becomes more popular all the time. The introduction of the Tornado to the Olympics in the 1960s triggered a catamaran explosion, and in recent years we have seen a tremendous diversification in catamaran design, ranging from beach cats made of polypropylene to hi-tech carbon fibre racing machines. Today there is a catamaran to suit every pocket and every need; the hardest part is deciding which design will suit your particular style of racing.

Each design has its own strengths and weaknesses, and each has inspired the development of sailing techniques specific to that boat. Our aim here is not to explain those techniques in detail but to pass on an approach to catamaran racing that has worked for us regardless of the class we have been sailing in.

There is no magic to winning, but there is a winning formula. You need to sort out the boat *in detail*, so everything works perfectly and nothing is left to chance in a race. You need to sort out your sailing, so speed is almost automatic. And you need a plan of action.

This book is about devising that plan, and following it through in an unwavering and single-minded way. Who knows, it may one day help you win a local, national, or even World title, as it did for us.

Our philosophy of combining a game plan with thorough preparation overflowed into our everyday way of thinking, and into our business and personal lives to a degree we would never have thought possible. It worked for us and we hope it works for you. Good luck and good racing!

☛ The authors: Kim Furniss (left) and Sarah Powell.

PART ONE

SPEED SAILING

SAIL TRIM

To go fast you must make the air flow properly across the sails. Without that, you're not going to get far.

Wind indicators and telltales

You can't see the wind, but a wind indicator and a set of telltales can show what it's doing.

On a cat, a burgee at the masthead is not accurate enough. You need an indicator on the bridle wire: it is useful upwind and essential downwind when you're trying to find the best course relative to the wind.

All cats should also have telltales to act as guides to airflow across the sails. They can be strands of wool knotted through the sail, or lengths of lightweight tape. Don't underestimate them because they are simple: reading the telltales and understanding their message is critical to sail trim.

To set the jib sail the boat to windward and watch the telltales. The sail is set properly when both the windward and the leeward telltales are flowing horizontally. If the jibsheet is too tight the top leeward telltale will stall – that is flow up or down, or jiggle in a circle. If you oversheet

◄ Use the jib telltales on the beat. If the top leeward telltale is stalled (left) the sheet is too tight, while if the windward telltales are stalled (centre) the sheet is too loose. The setting is correct when all the telltales are flowing (right).

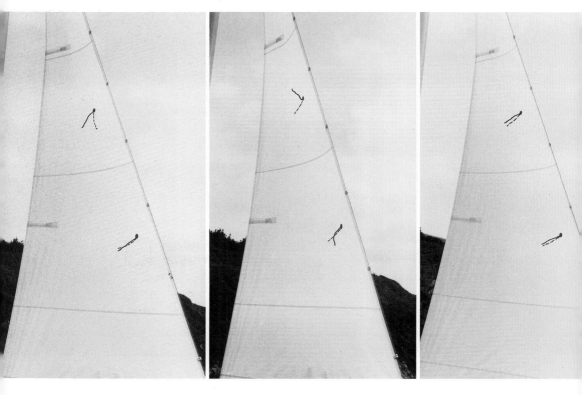

even more the lower leeward telltale will stall too. If the jibsheet is too loose the windward telltales will stall. Try it, and practise getting it right.

You can also use the jib telltales to help you position the jib fairleads. Put the boat on a beat and set the jibsheet so the telltales are flowing. Now luff slowly: if the top (windward) telltale stalls before the bottom one the sail is too twisted, so move the fairlead forwards. If the bottom (windward) telltale breaks first the sail is not twisted enough to move the fairlead aft.

On the mainsail the most important telltale is on the leeward side, approximately one quarter of the way down from the head. As with the jib, this telltale should be flowing horizontally. Haul in the mainsheet, and when the telltale stalls ease the sheet slightly until it flows horizontally again. This will give you the correct setting for optimum airflow across the sail.

You need to be aware of your class rules. Some allow as many telltales as you like but some one-design classes have strict rules about where telltales can be placed on the mainsail and jib. It is better to have a few in the right position rather than so many that you become confused about the information they are giving you.

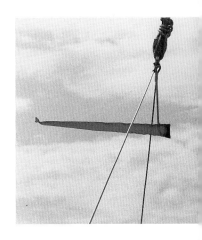

◆ The bridle wire indicator, blowing dead downwind.

◆ Upwind, pull in the main until the top leeward telltale stalls (left); then ease the sheet until it flows again (right).

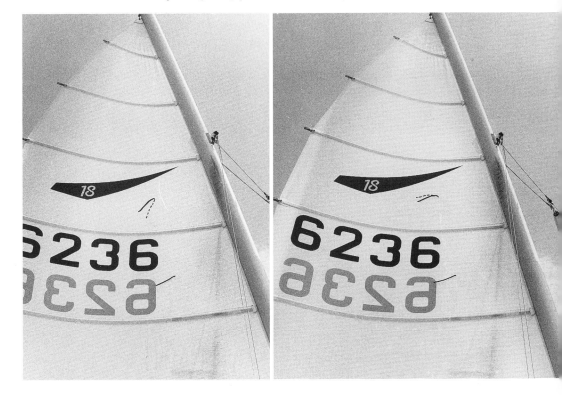

Sail Shape

In light airs you should keep the main and jibsheets loose to keep the leeches soft for good airflow across the sails.

As the wind increases you can get more speed and power by having slightly fuller sails. You can achieve this by:
- increasing batten tension
- keeping the downhaul slack
- using softer battens (if the class rules allow).

If you are having to spill wind to keep the boat flat, you should flatten the sails to allow the air to move across them faster. To flatten a sail on a catamaran with a boom, tension the outhaul and downhaul to their maximum setting, and increase pre-bend on the mast. If your class rules permit it, use stiffer battens (on a Hurricane turn the top two battens end-for-end). If your boat has no boom:
- slacken the battens so they are almost loose in their pockets
- increase the downhaul tension.

The jib slot

Don't ignore the jib just because of its size. Not only does it generate power in its own right, but it directs wind around the back of the mainsail: this is called the slot effect.

The effect of the downhaul of a Tornado: tensioned to flatten the sail (left), and then released (right).

◆ In strong winds slide the block back and outboard to open the slot and slacken the leech.

◆ For medium airs tighten the leech and close the slot by moving the block forward and inboard.

◆ In light airs move the block back and outboard a little to open the leech and keep the air flowing.

If the jibsheet is too tight the slot is choked and airflow will be reduced around the lee of the main. If the jibsheet is too loose the slot effect will be lost. Unfortunately, with a fully battened main, the mainsail won't show you how the slot is working; you will have to rely on checking your speed against the fleet.

Jib fairlead positions

Move the fairleads aft in light airs to open the jib leech, and move the fairleads forward as the wind increases to tighten the leech. In very strong winds move the fairleads aft and/or outboard to slacken the leech and open the slot. Mark two or three positions on the fairlead tracks to give you a setting guide for the different wind strengths.

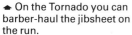 On the Tornado you can barber-haul the jibsheet on the run.

◄ On other cats such as the Dart the crew has to barber-haul the jibsheet manually on a light or medium-air run.

◗ We set the jib fairleads of the Dart some 34 inches from the forward beam. This puts sufficient depth and twist in the top of the sail, and we rarely need to move them.

← On the Dart the jib tack rope is critical to pointing. Here it is too loose.

← Here the jib tack is too tight – notice the crease it has pulled into the luff of the sail.

← Here it is just right.
← Set the mainsheet tension for the wind strength, then adjust the tack and tie it.

Setting the mainsail leech

Ideally the leech of the main should point aft, parallel to the centreline of the boat. Look at the leech about two-thirds of the way up the sail and adjust the mainsheet until it's right.

Too much mainsheet tension will give a hooked leech, which is slow: if that critical area two-thirds of the way up points to windward of the centreline it destroys the airflow. The boat may point in the right direction on a beat, but your speed will suffer and you'll make leeway.

Conversely, insufficient mainsheet tension gives an open leech, and pointing suffers. But there are a few cases where pointing isn't everything: in a choppy sea, for example, or when accelerating off the startline.

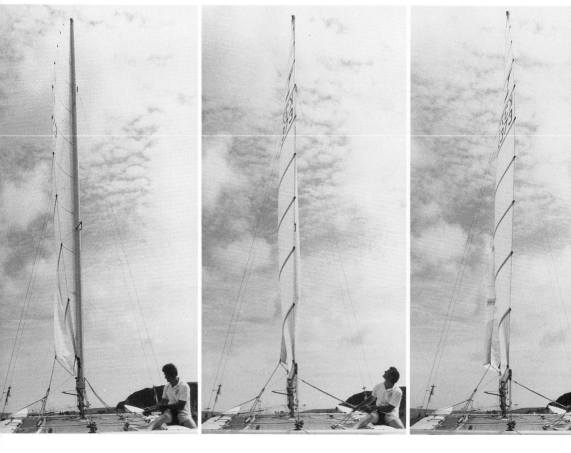

◆ In light airs open the mainsail leech to keep the air flowing (left). Tighten it in medium airs (centre), and in strong winds just pull the mainsheet on as hard as you can (right); the wind will blow the sail out to the correct position. If necessary ease the main a little to open the leech and let the air blast through.

A hooked leech may also be caused by too much downhaul tension, which increases mast bend. In light airs keep downhaul tension to the minimum allowed by the cut of your sail: just enough to lightly smooth out any wrinkles. However, some cats such as the Hurricane will need more downhaul tension.

Using the traveller

You can use the traveller to balance the boat without compromising performance. For example, as the wind increases and you need to spill wind from the mainsail to keep the boat flat, ease the traveller off-centre. This enables you to maintain good mainsheet tension, which keeps the forestay tight and helps the boat point.

In stronger winds try dropping the traveller down a larage amount and see how the boat feels. You will soon find the best position for each wind strength. Mark these positions on the track and use them as reference points when sailing.

Mast rotation

Rotating the mast away from the centreline increases the fullness of the mainsail. Conversely, reducing the rotation of the mast flattens the sail. If the rig has spreaders, more tension on the spreader wires will increase mast bend and also help to flatten the sail, further reducing power.

➤ If you need to spill a little wind on the beat, ease the traveller while keeping the sheet tight to maintain the sail shape.

➤ Rotate the mast to increase the fullness of the mainsail.

➤ Less rotation flattens off the sail and depowers it.

THE CREWING PARTNERSHIP

Crewing together is like a business partnership. It can work well or the participants can end up at loggerheads. Our partnership was successful because we shared the same goals: we were hungry to win but also shared the same philosophy about losing. We had the same commitment but realised that the most important thing was to keep a happy and fun boat. If there is any element of discord between the helm and crew you are beaten before you begin – it destroys your concentration and ultimately it will destroy your regatta results. Winning is fun, but you cannot win all the time so enjoyment is of paramount importance. If you don't enjoy sailing with your partner you should find someone else.

You must have good communication and a clear understanding of who gives the commands on the boat. You will have to keep them simple because you will often have to make split-second decisions and you will need to move fast. Therefore you will need to know exactly what is implied by every command, and put it into action immediately.

➤ You need to think and act together to sail the boat to her full potential, so good crew communication is vital.

Crew skills

The crew can also give an enormous amount of useful information to the helmsman while he is concentrating on boatspeed and tactics. Don't forget that it's a business partnership – and sailing fast is your business.

The crew should always study the sailing instructions and know exactly what the course is. He should also note any amendments to the sailing instructions.

It is better for the crew to be the timekeeper and take responsibility for the starting sequence, since this leaves the helmsman free to concentrate on other aspects of your game plan.

After the start of a race, the crew should be watching to see which boats go left or right up the first beat and the advantages they are gaining. He should also be aware of any windshifts.

The crew must move his weight fore and aft when on the trapeze, moving forward as the wind drops off and moving aft as the wind increases. These changes may not be obvious to the crew, so the helmsman should tell him in good time before any speed is lost.

The crew should constantly check on sail trim, hull trim and the performance of other boats in the fleet.

Weight distribution

The weight distribution of the helmsman and crew is critical. It makes the difference between going slowly or getting in the groove and going fast.

It is difficult to describe how to get a catamaran 'in the groove', except to say that you will know when you are there! It comes with practice and instinct; once you have it sorted out it's a great feeling – powering up the beat, sailing past other competitors and picking off places!

Less experienced sailors can use the (painted) waterline on the hulls to put their weight in roughly the right position. Aim to have the waterline parallel to the water. If your weight is too far forward the rudders will stall and the boat will be difficult to steer. In a seaway the bows may bury and cause additional drag. Conversely if you are too far back the transom will drag. This will be apparent from the noise coming from the back of the boat. The bows will be riding high and not cutting through the water cleanly.

The way you move around the boat is also important, particularly in light winds when you must stay as still as possible. Unnecessary movement causes interruption of the airflow across the sail and will affect your boatspeed.

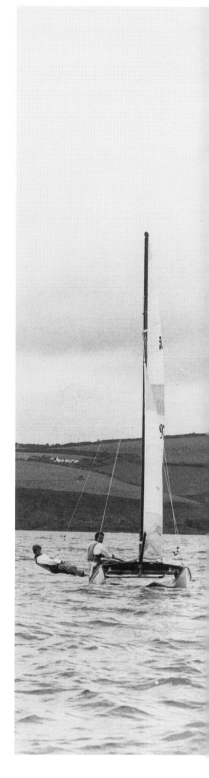

TRAPEZING

You will be racing on large courses, so let's start with comfort: if you are not comfortable on the wire you will be at an immediate disadvantage. The design of trapeze harnesses has been gradually improved to make them more comfortable. There are three main types of harness which we would recommend for racing catamarans:
● the spreader design with thigh straps and plastic buckles
● the made-to-measure 'nappy style'
● the original lace-up system.
Whatever harness you choose make sure it is comfortable and fits you well. If in doubt, try another style. A good trapeze harness will see you through many years of sailing.

Your harness should be as tight as possible around the hips, either laced or strapped firmly to your body. The harness hook should be lower rather than higher: in line with your hips and not your waist. On a new harness make sure you cut off the rubber grommet that lies beneath the harness hook. To tack fast you need to disconnect yourself with a downward movement of the arm and the rubber grommet makes this manoeuvre too slow.

➤ Make sure you are comfortable on the wire. If the harness is the wrong style you will be reluctant to use your weight to full advantage.

Trapezing technique

Always set and check the trapeze hook on the boat before going afloat. It does not have to be exact, but near enough. The general rule is that the lower you trapeze, the more leverage you get. So if it is windy, with flat water, set the hook low to give a horizontal trapezing position. If it is windy but with a lumpy sea, set it at a medium height. If the wind is light, set the hook at a higher level and trapeze with slightly bent knees.

These levels will become apparent only with practice out on the water. If necessary mark the trapeze rope with an indelible pen and use the marks as reference points. If in doubt 'go low' – you will soon realise that if you get hit by a wave you need to increase your height!

If you have a twin-wire boat it is always best for the crew to trapeze lower than the helmsman. This enables the helmsman to see over the top of his crew to check on other boats and to watch the wave pattern.

On a twin-wire boat it is normal for the helmsman to wire first and for the crew to do any balancing of the boat by moving on or off the wire. It is better for the crew to do the fine balancing because the helmsman has the mainsheet and tiller extension to concentrate on.

◄ On a twin-trapeze boat the helm can stay on the wire and concentrate on steering, while the crew maintains the balance by moving in and out as necessary.

◄ A practice run: trim the jib, cleat it and hook on . . .   Get your bottom over the side . . .

Always aim to have a trial run up the first beat on both port and starboard tacks to get the trapeze set at a near-perfect height. You will not have time to keep altering it while racing so get it ready before the start. In shifting conditions you may wish to make slight alterations to your height, or even at the start of a reach, but be careful not to become so preoccupied with adjustments that you forget the purpose of the race – to sail as fast as you possibly can.

Trapeze tips
● Trim the jib before going out on the wire. This is your power so keep driving every second of the way.
● Hook yourself on. Some catamarans have a block system incorporating shockcord which will help keep you

◄ To tack, check the jibsheets are not tangled, then grab the handle . . .   Move inboard, keeping your sheet hand in a constant position . . .

Push out with both feet . . .

And angle your front foot forward to stop you slipping forward.

attached to the hook until your body weight is suspended. On others, such as the Dart, you will have to make sure you are still connected as you leave the side deck. There is nothing more embarrassing than confidently throwing yourself out on the wire only to discover you have become disconnected!

● Drop your weight over the edge of the side deck and let the wire take up the slack.

● Your aim is to push out with both your legs simultaneously, keeping level with the deck (unless you're on a high wire in light winds). The quicker you get out on the trapeze wire the faster you will sail.

● Once you're out, check the trim of the sails.

● Trapeze on the balls of your feet and use your knees as

Once your weight is on the hull, unhook and move onto the trampoline . . .

Cross the boat, pulling in the new jibsheet as you go.

◆ You need to adjust your position constantly to keep the balance right, so . . .

In a lull, bend your legs and move forward to keep the windward hull flying.

Then as the wind increases move out again . . .

◆ When you move forward you will need to transfer the sheet around the shroud.

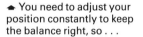

shock absorbers. Trapezing on your heels in a rough sea is uncomfortable and won't help your balance.

● If you have trouble staying on the boat, lock one knee. Which knee (front or back) depends on the catamaran you're sailing, because mast rake varies from class to class.

● When the hull flies high and the angle of the mast pulls you inboard towards the sail, bend your knees and ease off the jib. This will have the effect of flattening the boat, reducing the acute trapezing angle and saving a capsize.

● The trapeze handle may seem like a lifeline but should only be used as a means of getting in and out onto the wire. Lie back and maintain that low driving position, using your weight for maximum leverage. If you are trapezing at the right height you will not be within easy reach of the handle.

● Keep your arms by your side so you can trim the sails and operate the rig controls.

● Keep your feet as close together as reasonably possible.

● As you become more confident, you will use toe loops less and less. They make minute movements of body weight along the hull side impossible, and make a quick tack difficult. Practice without – it will pay dividends in the end. Their best function, especially on a Dart, is as handles to hold onto when gybing in very rough and windy conditions, so you don't get thrown off the side when the sail bangs over. They're also great for stopping your weight going forward when you are sailing downwind.

And 'walk' back along the hull to shift the weight aft. Avoid the toe loops.

Note that when you are aft you straighten your forward leg, and vice versa.

The total distance between the forward and aft positions varies from boat to boat – it may be 5 feet on a Hobie 16 or 9 feet on a Tornado.

● Never trapeze without boots. On strict one-designs you are not allowed to put extra anti-slip on the deck side and boots help keep you on your feet.

● Trapezing too high makes getting out on the wire awkward and slow. The hook should not be taking all your weight until you are over the edge of the boat. If it takes your weight as you sit on the deck then the setting is too high.

◄ Trapeze low and flat for maximum leverage, sea conditions permitting.

◆ Bottom over the side . . .

Push yourself out . . .

◆ Time to come in, so . . .

Grab the handle, swing inboard while keeping
the sheet tight . . .

Get both feet secure . . .

Then let go the handle and stretch out.

Unhook, get settled and secure . . .

And trim the jib.

BEATING IN MEDIUM WINDS

In medium winds the helm and crew should have their weight close together and far enough forward to prevent transom drag. Keep body movement to a minimum. The crew should be trapezing horizontally with his feet close together, bending his knees in the lulls and straightening his body in the gusts. In marginal trapezing conditions it is better for the helmsman and crew to hike hard, rather than kill boatspeed by moving in and out on the trapeze for short periods of time.

◀ A medium-wind beat, with the crew flat out on the wire.

Setting up the rig

Rig the mast in an upright position, with slightly reduced rotation to give maximum power all round the course.

The sails should be full to give maximum drive without excessive downhaul. The leech of the mainsail must be open and the traveller should be in the centre of the track. Tension the mainsheet enough to give the desired leech profile – it's right just before the telltales stall out. Be careful not to oversheet: a reference mark on the sheet will stop you anxiously pulling it in too tight when you're under pressure. If you have centreboards, fully extend them on both sides for maximum lateral resistance and pointing ability.

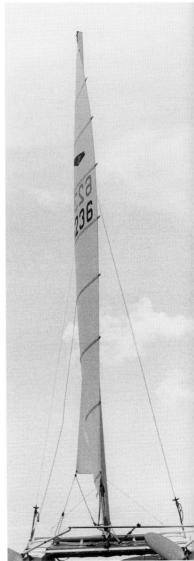

→ The main set up for medium airs (in practice the wind will blow it out further than this and open the leech).

Steering

Avoid excessive rudder movement because this just increases drag. You can hold the tiller extension in an under-arm or an over-arm grip, but our personal preference is for under-arm because it enables you to steer the boat smoothly using your shoulder while keeping both hands free to work the mainsheet. You hug the tiller extension tight to your armpit and steer the boat through small waves and gusts by rotating your upper body.

Many successful sailors use the over-arm method, but it is more of a dinghy grip; it makes sheeting awkward and does not give a positive locking position for the tiller extension.

→ Steering with the tiller extension held under-arm allows you to grip it in your armpit while using both hands to work the mainsheet.

How can I make the boat point?

Get good boatspeed before you ask the boat to point higher. Avoid excessive heeling by trimming the sails so the windward hull skims the tops of the waves and does not fly too high.

The stronger the wind the tighter the luff tension on the jib should be, reducing the fullness in the sail.

Set your fairleads for maximum power by pulling the jib in tight and easing off slowly. If the top telltale stalls first move the fairleads further forward so that when the sail is eased off the telltales both stall at the same time. There is a tendency to oversheet the jib. If the leeward telltale starts to flow upwards ease the jib; millimetres can make all the difference to your boatspeed.

The jib blocks on a Dart should be set so they are difficult to cleat: this makes minute sail adjustments easier. Catamarans with bigger jibs may not give you this option.

BEATING IN LIGHT WINDS

The helm and crew should have their weight as far forward and as close together as possible to lift the transoms out of the water. If conditions permit trapezing the crew should usually stay in front of the shroud. If the wind becomes too light to trapeze the crew should sit in front of the main beam to avoid too much transom drag. If the wind becomes even lighter the crew should lie down on or near the leeward hull. This spreads the weight over both hulls, which reduces transom drag. In the forward or leeward position it is not always easy to control the jib; if

◆ A light-air beat, with helm and crew close together and well forward to prevent transom drag.

◗ In a real drifter the crew should lie across the trampoline to spread the weight over both hulls.

so, the crew should pass the sheet to the helmsman. There should be no body movement except for (minimal) steering. So get comfortable, sit still, concentrate and watch the water for wind patterns and windshifts. Aim to sail towards the wind but avoid pinching. In marginal trapezing conditions it is better for the crew to hike out rather than move in and out on the trapeze. This prevents too much movement on the boat. It is faster to sail with the windward hull skimming the tops of the waves.

Trim the jib luff before going afloat: use light luff tension.

Move the fairleads well aft to open the jib leech and speed the airflow through the slot. Do not oversheet, and avoid excessive trimming of the sails which will disrupt the airflow. Switch off the ratchet system on the jib blocks for more precise sail trimming.

On the Dart mainsail luff tension should be light to prevent the leech hooking. On other cats the downhaul has a different effect, and can be used to flatten the sail to increase the airflow. The mast should be upright to give power, and if in doubt it is better to under-rotate the mast to give a flatter sail.

The traveller should be central. Take care not to oversheet the mainsheet and close the leech; markers for reference will help avoid this. Check your telltales and keep them flowing horizontally. If you oversheet you will lose forward momentum and skid sideways. If it helps, disengage the mainsheet ratchet system.

The centreboards should be down, but in certain conditions the windward board can be lifted to reduce drag. Only experience will tell you when this increases boatspeed. Find a tuning partner and practice.

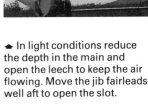

◆ In light conditions reduce the depth in the main and open the leech to keep the air flowing. Move the jib fairleads well aft to open the slot.

◆ A very light beat in a Hobie 16. The technique is the same as in the Dart (opposite).

BEATING IN STRONG WINDS

Whether you are lightweights or heavyweights, sailing in a strong breeze should be fun! Successful sailing in these conditions depends largely on your mental attitude. If you never try strong-wind sailing you will never discover the fun you are missing, so be positive, put those misgivings out of your mind and give it a go! Take it easy, going out for short bursts at a time so your confidence in boat handling grows.

In strong winds the helm and crew should move further aft and stay close together. The helmsman should be hiking out as straight-legged as possible, and the crew trapezing as low as possible in the sea conditions.

◗ A strong-wind beat in the Dart. As the hull starts to fly, ease the sheets to keep it kissing the water and achieve maximum boatspeed.

◀ Helm hiked out, crew trapezing flat and well aft, jib slot well open.

◀ The mainsail set up for a strong breeze. The leech is tight, but open enough to let the air escape easily.

When trapezing, your feet should be slightly further apart to maintain good contact with the boat, if necessary using one toe loop as an anchor point. Lock your knees and watch the waves. Use your body weight to help ease the boat over the waves, using your knees as shock absorbers for the impact. Hold the jibsheet for extra stability, but avoid cleating the jibsheet for safety. Move the jib fairleads further aft to open up the jib slot and let the air blast through.

In strong winds you will need to steer more vigorously as you work the boat through the wave pattern. As you sail into a gust and the windward hull starts to fly, ease the sheets. Then, as the hull comes down, re-trim the sails. This is a continuous process of hauling in and easing out the sheets, driving the boat up the beat. Avoid sailing with a high-flying hull, since this will only reduce boatspeed.

The helm and crew should work together, trimming the sails simultaneously in gusty conditions. You must aim for a steady, controlled easing off and sheeting in of sails. If you both 'dump' the sails together the boat will lose speed and may even lose momentum altogether. The helm should watch the crew: as the boat heels the crew should ease the jib gradually, and if the boat carries on heeling, the helm must then ease his mainsheet. As the heeling is reduced the helm should sheet in, followed by the crew, to achieve maximum power once more. (On a Hurricane or Tornado you cleat the jib and play the mainsheet and downhaul to keep the boat on its feet.)

If you feel the conditions are going to overpower you, increase the mast rake and fully rotate the mast. This will de-power the rig and, by moving the centre of effort aft, making boat handling easier. The boat can also be made

more manageable by sailing with a more open mainsail leech. (On a Dart a spanner line of maximum length, within the class rules, is vital for maximum mast rotation).

A mast without spreaders, such as that of the Dart, may counter-rotate and invert in strong winds. It has the appearance of bending the wrong way and if this is not rectified immediately the mast may suffer permanent damage. To get out of trouble release the jib sheets, sheet the main in tight and bear away; meanwhile the crew should come off the wire and push the spanner through to the correct side.

Ease the traveller to leeward from the centreline; this enables you to use greater mainsheet tension without heeling the boat excessively. The stronger the wind the further you have to ease the traveller off the centreline. This has the effect of making the boat easier to handle and not so sensitive in strong gusts. With good mainsheet tension the boat can be driven hard and an advantage can be gained by continuously working the sails without losing pointing ability and speed.

◀ In strong winds ease the traveller. This allows you to put greater tension on the mainsheet to maintain sail shape and pointing ability.

HOBIE SPECIFICS

The Hobie 16 has what we nicknamed 'the lifeline' – a rope
going around the boat just below the trampoline. It looks
cumbersome with its knots at intervals along its length, but
it makes sailing in heavy weather sheer bliss. Just lock
your knees, jib sheet in one hand, 'lifeline' in the other, and
you can sail all day in the roughest of seas without
worrying about getting washed off the boat.

As soon as you start to become overpowered, ease the
jib traveller about one third of the way. If you are still
overpowered start moving the main traveller out further. If
the main is being backwinded, ease the jib traveller more.
Keep moving the main out until your backside is in the
water, then sheet in an inch or two.

In strong conditions, the jib traveller will be all the way
out, and the main out to the hiking straps.

All the time the main and jib should be sheeted in tight.
It is much better to sheet in and travel out than the
reverse.

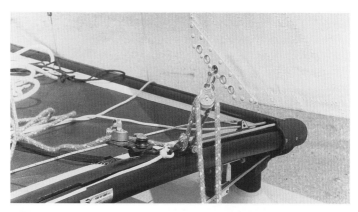

◗ The Hobie jib traveller in the
basic beating position.

◗ The jib traveller barber-
hauled to the end of its track
for the run.

◀ On a Hobie 16 it is important to sail with a lot of mast rake, so the mainsheet comes block to block. This is the medium wind setting; for strong winds we would rake the mast back further to open the leech even more.

The mainsheet block-to-block for beating, with the traveller central. The traveller is let off for the reach, and the sheet eased slightly (bottom).

REACHING IN MEDIUM WINDS

The helmsman and crew should move aft to prevent the bow burying, and keep their weight close together to reduce wind resistance and prevent pitching.

The crew should make use of the restraining line: in medium winds it's best to just hold the end of the line in the palm of your hand, constantly adjusting your body weight by moving forward in the lulls and aft in the gusts while adjusting the jibsheet.

The helmsman should keep the tiller under his arm so he can adjust the mainsheet rapidly. The aim is to keep the windward hull skimming over the tops of the waves, to avoid excessive heeling in the gusts and to ease off the mainsheet quickly if the bow starts to bury.

Twist is caused by easing off the mainsheet while leaving the traveller cleated in a central position. So move the traveller down to six inches (15 cm) below the centreline. Then pull in the mainsheet to give a tight leech with the right amount of twist.

◆ If you ease the mainsheet and keep the traveller central you get too much twist in the main for efficient reaching (left), so keep the main tight and let off the traveller to maintain the sail shape (right).

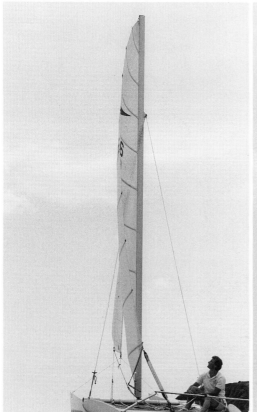

Keep playing the mainsheet and work the gusts. Bear away and drive off in the gusts, heading back to a proper course in the lulls. The more you work at the mainsheet the more drive you will get and the more likely you are to pass boats down the reach.

Mast rotation should be at its maximum setting. If you have centreboards, keep the windward one up and the leeward one down.

◀ Powering down the reach with the crew well aft and close together to reduce wind resistance.

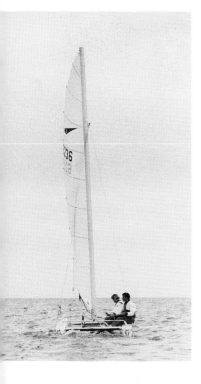

REACHING IN LIGHT WINDS

As when beating in light winds, move your weight well forward and sit close together. There should be hardly any movement on board to avoid disrupting the airflow across the sails.

Keep the mainsail leech open with maximum fullness at the foot of the sail. Rotate the mast to its maximum setting.

Steer slowly and keep rudder movement to a minimum: you don't want to kill the little way you have.

The deeper (further downwind) the reach the further outboard the fairleads must go, keeping them well forward.

Make full use of the barber-haulers to pull the jibsheets outboard and open the slot. If you don't have barber-haulers, the crew should hold the jibsheet blocks in one hand, setting the jib in the correct position and constantly re-trimming by watching the telltales to make sure they are flowing horizontally across the sail.

↑ A medium-light reach in the Dart, with the traveller down, the mast fully rotated and the mainsheet eased to keep the leech open.

→ In these fairly light conditions both crew are on the windward hull but sitting well inboard, forward and close together.

◀ The Hobie in really light airs, with the helm holding the boom out.

◀ In a drifter the crew should sit on the leeward hull to keep the boat balanced. On this Hobie 16 the jib is barber-hauled outboard to open the slot.

REACHING IN STRONG WINDS

What we've all been waiting for! Reaching in strong winds is the most exhilarating experience: it's fast and you're living on the edge. A moment's loss of concentration and your first place could be history. Stay sharp. The more effort you put into the reach the faster you'll go. Work those sails and give it all your energy and you will be rewarded.

At a World Championship in 1991 we took off down the reach with 300 boats behind us. It was a magnificent sight – we just looked back in awe! Imagine the joy of being able to sail your own course. We could sail our own course, directly to the next mark, while everyone else had to fight for clear air.

◆ Trapezing 'piggy-back' behind the helmsman to keep the weight well aft.

The helmsman and crew *must* be well aft, if necessary with the crew trapezing 'piggy back' on the restraining line behind the helmsman. It makes life easier sometimes if the helmsman passes the tiller to the crew while he works the mainsheet. On a twin trapeze boat it may be better for the helm to sit in and leave the crew out on the wire.

Because of the tendency to nosedive, it's safer for the crew to use the rear toe-loop to stop himself being thrown forward if the bows digs in. Keep the boat balanced with positive footwork.

Your steering must also be positive: steer around the waves and drive off in strong gusts. If the waves are really large steer up and over, driving off the face and flying a hull over the crest if necessary. Using waves to your advantage can significantly increase your boatspeed.

Work the sails simultaneously, avoiding dumping the power altogether.

On a strong-wind reach the traveller can be eased as much as 12 inches (30 cm) to help control the twist of the mainsail. To go really fast work the mainsheet double-handed, keeping the tiller under your arm and steering by moving your shoulder.

◀ The restraining line stops the crew swinging forward from the aft position. Note the way the traveller has been eased to control mainsail twist.

← Aaaaargh!

← Keep playing the jib. If in doubt, dump it completely. You're meant to be sailing, not swimming . . .

THE NOSEDIVE

Nosediving or cartwheeling is one of those things that happens to most cat sailors at some time. It's really no big deal, but the apres-sail tales in the bar afterwards get more elaborate and spectacular after each round of drinks!

A nosedive is controllable, survivable and (usually) preventable. It's important to know how and why it happens, and what to do when it does.

You will nosedive if:

● your catamaran has little buoyancy in the bows. For example it does not take much to make a Dart nosedive, whereas a Tornado or Hurricane is more forgiving and you will have several chances before you need a snorkel
● you have too much power in the sails
● you are too far forward, or too far apart
● you steer straight into a big wave
● you don't react to a gust.

So to stay on an even keel:

● watch the bows – this is critical
● ease the jib immediately the bows start to dip
● if the bows still dip, dump the jib completely
● if you're still heading for a nosedive, dump the main
● move back, and keep close together. At all costs you must keep aft
● steer round waves
● bear away in fierce gusts.

THE RUN — MEDIUM WINDS

The aim of the downwind leg is to sail as low as you can to reduce your distance, but without foregoing any speed. The most successful downwind sailors are those who have the greatest sense of speed differential.

The helmsman and crew should be on the same side of the boat and as far forward as possible. The aim is to balance the boat and avoid transom drag, but without the bows dipping in. If the bows start to bury just move your weight back a little to re-trim the hull.

Depending on the catamaran you sail you will have the benefit of either a bridle telltale or a wind indicator. A wind indicator such as a Windex is more accurate than a telltale but is based on the same principle. Both tell you your tacking angle and how deep downwind to sail. The ideal varies from boat to boat but, as a guide, the bridle telltale should be aiming at the leeward bridle wire.

Downwind you must learn to exploit the gusts. In stronger wind bear away to go deeper, and as the wind drops off come back gradually to your normal course (all turns must be slow, or you will lose speed). This technique takes practice, but is well worth perfecting because it shortens the distance from buoy to buoy.

Use the waves to your advantage, sailing higher to catch a wave and then bearing away to increase speed as you sail down the face. This also helps you sail deep, before luffing to keep your speed up and look for the next wave.

◆ Keep well forward on the run, but move aft and ease the jibsheet if the leeward hull starts to dip.

◆ Let the traveller right down to control twist.

▶ The Hobie jib can be barber-hauled to the end of its track to control the jib leech.

➡ Keep the mast rotated and the sails full for speed.

Set the barber-haulers well outboard because this stops the jib leech twisting off and helps to keep the power in the sail. On catamarans without barber-haulers the crew will have to set the jib manually, reading the wind through the telltales. To do this, hold the jib blocks and move your hand forward (tightening the leech) or backward (tightening the foot) until you're happy with the shape. Moving your hand inboard or outboard controls the telltales. Note that it pays for the crew to set the jib early as you go through each gybe.

The mast should be fully rotated to keep the sail full. On catamarans without a sophisticated mast rotation system, you will have to exert pressure on the mast spanner to prevent the movement of the boat swinging the spanner and interrupting the airflow.

Let the traveller run its full course, except on wide-beamed catamarans such as the Tornado when this can be excessive. On such boats the movement across the track should be restricted.

Ease the mainsheet sufficiently to create twist and good airflow; keep a careful eye on the leeward telltales.

THE RUN – LIGHT WINDS

The helmsman and crew should be on opposite sides of the boat with their weight well forward and sitting as still as possible: this not only prevents disruption of the airflow but avoids turbulence in the water. If the crew weight is not separated one hull may submerge and cause unnecessary drag. In a rolling sea you can prevent rudder slop by gripping the tiller firmly against your body.

A light-wind run on the Hobie, with the helm and crew holding the sails out.

It helps if the helm or crew puts his foot on the spanner at the base of the mast to prevent mast movement. The crew should have his back to the shroud to take the slack out of the rig; this is especially beneficial on a Dart.

The mainsheet should be very slack to keep the telltales flowing correctly. You may need to hold the boom outboard.

In light airs concentration on the jib is critical, so keep your eyes on the telltales. In this situation the crew has a good feeling for the wind strength and direction through the jib and should relate this information to the helmsman, telling him when he can sail a lower course.

The Dart, with mast well rotated to give a full sail.

Here the crew is manually barber-hauling the jib, holding the spanner across with her foot and tensioning the leeward shroud by leaning against it.

▲ Stay well back in strong winds; the crew may need to cling to a toe loop.

▲ Keeping the crew weight well aft should stop the bows from burying – but be ready to dump the jib if they dip into the danger zone.

THE RUN – STRONG WINDS

In a strong wind running is exciting because there is always the possibility of a nosedive. Most of your energies will be devoted to preventing this.

Your weight should be aft – by the rear beam. You must not be pushed forward so hold on to either a toestrap, a toe loop or even the restraining line (the crew will need to reach behind the helmsman with his back hand).

Sit still and concentrate on the sails and the position of the bows in the water. With experience you will get a mental picture of how far the bows can dip without risking a nosedive. The crew must coordinate his hands and eyes, and immediately the bow goes into the danger zone, ease the jib. Remember: staying upright depends on this! Your reactions must be fast.

We always say to people 'if in doubt dump the jib'. Don't be afraid to let if flog – if you're fighting to stay upright boatspeed, for once, is of less importance. Be cautious and stay upright! In strong winds sail with an older jib so you won't be reluctant to let it flog.

In survival conditions it pays to sail far lower than normal. Pick your moment in the wave and gust pattern and bear away onto the new heading, at the same time sheeting in the mainsail. This has the effect of reversing the airflow across the mainsail, which makes the boat slow down and become more manageable. And because the jib is now in the shadow of the mainsail its power is reduced, which lessens the risk of a nosedive.

Assuming you're running normally, **bear away when a heavy gust strikes.** This is essential for survival.

Take care when you gybe. The procedure is as described later but you must carve a much shallower turn. If you try to turn too fast the airflow will return to its original path across the sail, and you'll execute a catastrophic nosedive!

◆ Bear away in the gusts, or you'll be swimming.

◆ Get some speed . . .

Feed the rudder blades into the turn . . .

And keep the rudders at 45 degrees.

TACKING IN MEDIUM WINDS

Whichever class of catamaran you sail you will need to practise tacking. If you tack badly it is a slow, cumbersome manoeuvre, but a series of slick tacks can help you gain advantage over your competitors.

The problems of tacking a catamaran are caused by one hull having to travel a greater distance, as well as the length of the waterline. Also, because of its light construction, there is insufficient momentum to help the boat through its tack – unlike say a keelboat. The solution to these problems is good boatspeed as you go into the tack, and a slow turn as you start the manoeuvre. (The flip side of this is that you can easily slow a catamaran by sharply turning one way then the other. This is especially useful when you want to slow down your approach to the startline, or in tight manoeuvres.)

Before tacking in medium winds the boat should be balanced and moving with good speed. Check that your sheets are not tangled.

It is essential to avoid moving your weight too far aft during a tack, except perhaps in a Tornado where, because the waterline is long, the bows need to be lifted through the eye of the wind to make a fast tack.

Crew crosses the boat, backs the jib . . .

And sheets in while the helm moves across . . .

Sheets in and accelerates away.

The helmsman should feed the rudder blades into the tack with a smooth positive push, without snatching. Push the rudder blades to 45 degrees only – any more will have the effect of slowing down the tack. Keep the blades like this throughout the tack: if they are centralised the progress of the tack will be stopped, so don't straighten the blades until the boat is on its new course.

For training purposes push the rudders across, then count to six before moving across the boat. This will roll the boat through the tack. Ease the mainsheet slightly in the middle of the tack.

The crew should come in off the wire and back the jib carefully until the nose of the boat moves round to the new tack, then sheet in and move out onto the trapeze.

Note that the crew moves earlier than the helmsman, moving across the trampoline (facing forwards), hooking on and moving out on the trapeze as the helmsman sits down and sheets in for acceleration.

If the crew feels the boat has lost some momentum as it goes into the tack he can compensate by keeping the jib backed a fraction longer and by keeping the sheet eased on the new heading, sheeting tighter as speed increases.

On the Hobie 16 you may have to bend the jib's battens to stop them getting caught on the mast in mid-tack.

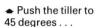
← Push the tiller to 45 degrees . . .

Wait while the boat comes round . . .

Back the jib . . .

TACKING IN LIGHT WINDS

The helmsman and crew should keep their weight well forward. The crew will probably already be sitting in the centre of the boat on the trampoline by the mast, so during a tack he merely needs to transfer the jib from one side to the other with slow, positive movements. Keep the jib backed for slightly longer than usual, until you are sure the nose of the boat has swung through the eye of what little wind there is and you are on your new tack. The crew should also rotate the mast manually when head-to-wind to speed up the airflow on the new tack.

Avoid any movement on the boat until it has clearly gone past head-to-wind: this is vital.

To begin the tack push the rudder blades to a 45 degree angle but no more. Any further will cost you speed. Swop the tiller from hand to hand at arms length so as to keep your body weight as far forward as possible. Ease the mainsheet slightly through the tack to help the boat accelerate afterwards.

On rigs without booms, the battens may have to be flipped by hand if the wind is too light to do the job. Push with one hand in the centre of the battens and pull with the other hand near the bottom batten.

TACKING IN STRONG WINDS

If you are anxious about tacking in strong winds, tack in the lulls and not in the full force of a gust. But if you are more confident, tacking in the gusts can help because you are already sailing as close to the wind as possible so the tacking angle is reduced.

Before starting a tack take a firm grip on the tiller and build up good boatspeed. The helmsman and crew should

Straighten up . . .   Change sides . . .   And sheet in.

both move their body weight back. In a big sea look for a
flat spot in the wave pattern. You will notice that they
frequently move in sets of three waves, followed by a lull.
Try to tack in this flat spot: it is better to sail a bit further
than risk tacking into a wave or, worse, in a trough. If there
are few flat spots aim to tack on the crest of a wave. What
you are looking for here is a second wave to push the
bows of the boat through onto the new tack. If you tack in a
trough the tack will be slow and it is almost certain you will
stop.

If you get into irons you can get out of trouble by
'reversing' the rudder blades. The boat will eventually go
backwards and turn until it is pointing in the right
direction. Then sheet in and accelerate away.

You can begin the tack with the crew still out on the
wire, although this needs practice and good coordination
between helmsman and crew. The crew can then use
the 'G-force' to come in off the wire. If you are not used to
this technique take care, or you will end up in a heap on
the trampoline! As a guide, in strong winds you need only
count to two before moving across the boat.

On a catamaran without centreboards backing the jib
for a short time helps the boat through the tack. The crew
must have both jibsheets held ready as you go into the
tack. He then moves across the boat taking the new
jibsheet with him, which leaves less rope to pull in and
allows for quicker setting of the jib. A catamaran with
centreboards doesn't need that extra help because it is
tacking on a pivot.

The helmsman should steer into the tack in a positive
manner, using a sharp push to start the turn. Ease the
mainsheet by 18–24 inches (45–60 cm) as you move across
the boat. This opens the leech, speeding the airflow over
the main on the new tack and helping acceleration. When
the boat is back up to speed, sheet in again.

⬤ Helm up . . .   Cross to the centre . . .   Swop hands . . .

GYBING IN MEDIUM WINDS

The helmsman and crew should have their weight in the middle of the boat, and fairly well forwards.

Start the gybe slowly, speeding up through the manoeuvre. The helmsman, in the centre of the boat, swops hands ready to pre-gybe the mainsail. When the boat is dead downwind the mainsail will become slack and this is the time to ease the sail across to the opposite side; don't wait until it bangs across of its own accord. Let the traveller run down the full length of its track.

There is a tendency for inexperienced sailors to let the rudders straighten up during the gybe. This slows the gybe down because you have then got to steer the boat

⬤ Gybing with the Hobie asymmetric kite.

Move the mainsheet across . . .   Straighten up as the sail cracks over . . .   And go!

back up onto the correct heading. The other error people make is to keep the blades locked over for too long, causing the boat to luff up after the gybe. You then waste time by having to bear away again. As a general rule, straighten the rudder blades as the sail cracks over.

The crew should also pre-set the jib on the new side, which saves time and helps keep up speed. He also needs to rotate the mast manually (unless a most rotation system is fitted) as he moves across the boat, a second before the battens crack over. This ensures the sail is set immediately on the new gybe.

You can use a small amount of centreboard, but be careful because too much will trip the boat up, causing a capsize.

◄ A light-air gybe: helm up . . .

Steady as she goes . . .

Crew pops the jib battens across . . .

GYBING IN LIGHT WINDS

The helmsman should be on the windward hull and the crew on the leeward hull, both with their weight well forward. As you change sides avoid too much movement because this just slows the boat down. A light-wind gybe should be a slow, graceful manoeuvre with a much slower start than in other wind strengths.

The traveller should be left to run its full length.

Once on the new gybe, it is easier for the helmsman to free off the old jibsheet. If necessary, he can flip the battens to their new position by pushing them through with one hand.

On catamarans with barber-haulers the crew should uncleat and re-set them as he crosses the boat. To speed up the gybe he can rotate the mast manually to increase boatspeed. This also helps the battens flip to their new setting.

GYBING IN STRONG WINDS

Apart from your own natural caution, the main problem during a heavy-air gybe is nosediving. Let's see how to prevent it.

Firstly, both helmsman and crew should be on the same side of the boat, *with their weight well aft* and alert for a nosedive – unless you are brave enough to experience 'The Wild Thing' developed by Australian World Tornado Champion, Mitch Booth, where the helm and crew sit on opposite sides of the boat and swop position in the middle of the gybe.

Helm crosses the boat . . .   Straightens up as the crew crosses   And away she goes.
                              the boat . . .

If you are out of control run straight downwind and sheet in so the boat slows down. Only gybe when you are under control.

In strong winds pre-gybing the mainsail is far more critical than in other wind strengths. If you let it follow its own course and slam across to the other side the impact is so great that the boat cannot accelerate fast enough and the bows are pushed down into a nosedive.

Turn smoothly through the gybe, gradually increasing the angle of the rudder blades. Straighten them up as the boat reaches its new course, otherwise they act as a brake

➥ A heavy-air gybe: go for a smooth, gradual turn – and watch the bows!

which can once again cause a nosedive as the boat tries to accelerate. The objective is a smooth, gradual turn.

The traveller, again, should be left to run its full course and the mainsheet should be left to run free.

Be careful when sheeting in after the gybe: keep watching for waves and checking the angle of the bows. If necessary 'dump' the jib for safety.

As the gybe starts the crew should move across the boat and, as a safety precaution, hold a toe loop or footstrap: there is a large 'G' force as the sail cracks across and the boat starts to accelerate.

PART TWO

RACE TACTICS

At all levels of sailing, thorough preparation is the key to success. If you organise yourself and your boat, you free yourself to concentrate on boatspeed, strategy and tactics.

When you arrive at the regatta be confident. Live in a way that suits you. Look after yourself. Success always demands an element of selfishness. Don't be influenced by others. Associating with slow, disenchanted sailors hinders your performance and erodes your positive way of thinking. What suits you may not suit the majority, but that's their problem.

Arrive early at major regattas and championships. Stick to your planned strategy, with its proven procedures and techniques. Do the necessary preliminary preparation at the regatta venue, such as registering your entry and getting the boat measured, but don't hang around the boat park every waking moment. Have a break from it; you will spend many hours sitting, tuning your boat, waiting to sail.

Aim for consistency. Championships can be won without winning a single race. Aim for good, consistent results in the top ten and you could be Number One!

PHYSICAL FITNESS

The amount of fitness training you do is up to you, but if you have had a series of six races in strong winds and ended up feeling exhausted you will realise that fitness is important. The fitter you are the more effort you can put into trapezing or the longer you can hike out, the faster you will go and in the end the less time you will spend out on the wire! We believe in fitness because it is something YOU can control.

It is hard to determine the level of fitness and the energy requirement you will need. Sailing isn't like running a 100 metres, when you know exactly what is going to happen. You might hang around at a regatta which has been blown off and use up very little energy, or there may be light winds for some races and very strong winds for others.

So how do you determine what you need to do? First, decide on your individual circumstances. What is your position on the boat? What is your lifestyle? How much time do you have free to sail? How fit do you want to be?

Next, remember that fitness is specific and should be measured in relation to a specific exercise. So even if you are the star of the aerobics class, you may not feel so good after a long, punishing beat in a force 6. The best way to get fit for sailing is to sail, but most people cannot sail every day. Sail as much as you can, but supplement this with some gym work, aiming for stamina building rather than heavy muscle gain. We tend to mountain-bike because it's fun, it's good for strengthening your legs and it improves stamina. Playing squash is good for your reactions, and swimming is good for overall body toning. Even a round of golf is relaxing, relieves the monotony and is good general exercise.

If you aren't fit your muscles may be pushed beyond their limit, which will cause pain and injury. This will not only hinder your performance physically but mentally too. Look after yourself and give your body a chance!

Try to warm up before the start. This helps injury and prepares the body for the physical and mental onslaught it's about to experience. If you don't have time to warm up before going afloat use the time sailing out to the start constructively. Keep moving, rotate and stretch your joints. Don't get cold: over-dress rather than skimp on clothing.

Also, if you warm *down* after the race it will help your muscles recover faster. Don't just slump in a chair in the

→ You can take this fitness thing a bit too far . . .

bar: do a few exercises to stretch your muscles and tendons to ensure they retain their flexibility.

Along with your fitness you need to consider your nutritional requirements. A good, healthy, sensible diet is an integral component in the preparation for competition.

Avoid eating fatty and junk food. Eat sensibly all year round including a diet of complex carbohydrates such as pasta, potatoes and bread. These do not cause weight gain when eaten with low-fat ingredients.

Don't change your diet suddenly before a regatta. At the event it is too late to worry about your weight or whether you are unfit. Plan your schedule of well-being a good way ahead and stick to what you decide.

Eat plenty of fresh food and go for protein in moderation. Drink plenty of fruit drinks and avoid dehydration. Immediately after the finish, start to restore your energy levels by eating a high-carbohydrate snack. The longer you wait to eat, the longer it will take to refuel your muscles, so don't wait for the bar to open but eat when or as you come ashore.

Be competitive, get fit, eat sensibly, feel good, stay sharp!

MENTAL ATTITUDE

There is more to racing success than blasting round the course: you also need to have your mind in gear. Regatta sailing is not primarily concerned with technical skill, because most of the sailors at such events are even on this score. The deciding factor is the ability to perform under pressure. Differences in boats will be marginal, especially in one-design sailing, and at the top end everyone will be fit. The winner will then be the person with the best mental attitude, a high level of commitment and a great deal of single-mindedness. So get ahead, get mentally fit!

Preparation is all-important. Begin by setting yourselves achievable short-term goals. These might include:
● Improving diet and getting fitter by doing some form of sport every day such as walking, running or swimming.
● Deciding how many times a week you can sail and what you want to practise. This could be as little as once a week. Remember such a plan has to be achievable.
● Embarking on a programme of psychological training: analysing and rationalising your way of thinking.

In this way you build up daily/weekly goals which will lead to a major objective – maybe yours will be to win a club race, an open meeting, a national or even a world event. Your ultimate goal will be to succeed at the level you have determined. Note that your goals are personal to you; they don't affect anyone else.

Setting yourself goals when training will improve your confidence. Practise with intensity so you feel comfortable and can perform under pressure. As you achieve a goal your self-confidence and motivation will increase, and your performance will improve.

Criticise your own performance, be objective and learn from experience. In this way you will profit from your mistakes, understand why you performed badly and gain something from each error.

Be careful not to set unrealistic goals and expect too much of yourself. This will only lead to failure. If you fail, start again from the beginning. Re-evaluate your performance and set yourself more comfortable, achievable goals. This will also help your stress level. Move slowly and not too ambitiously.

← Constantly analyse your performance and work on the weak aspects. There's always room for improvement.

A club sailor once said to us it was his aim to beat us at a national championship. He had only just moved to a catamaran from a monohull. He failed – he came last! But he persevered with his game plan and re-set himself realistic goals: to beat us in a club race. He succeeded. He then got a better placing at an open meeting and one day he'll probably be a national champion! If nothing else, this story highlights the benefit of realistic goal setting.

If you don't reach your goals, at whatever level you have set, don't be ashamed. Don't dwell on your failures, since this only increases the stress that comes with the desire to succeed. If you have prepared well but failed, you must find consolation that you gave it your best effort. Analyse why you failed and learn from the experience. Be prepared for the next time.

Keep searching for the way that will make YOU successful: work within your capabilities and in a way that suits your personality.

You must learn to concentrate and avoid distraction. Sailing is different from other sports, in that during a race you have to concentrate for extended periods. Learn to relax and put the race into perspective: tomorrow is another day, another race.

Learn to adjust to different environments. This is especially important at overseas regattas where different cultures are involved.

Develop the ability to cope with external pressures or adverse weather conditions that are out of your control.

If you get into trouble, put it behind you, get back into competitive mode and don't worry about the protests or arguments that may occur afterwards.

Think quickly and independently, especially about tactics.

Practice imagining. Imagine winning or achieving your goal. Imagine what will happen, how it will be. Some sailors are genuinely not comfortable with winning; they cannot visualise what it will be like and will sail to their own 'comfortable' level. Ask yourself whether you would like to do better? Are you comfortable at your current level? Would you be comfortable at a higher level?

You need to be confident that you can sail on 'auto-pilot' using your subconscious mind, and leaving your conscious mind free to consider tactics and the natural elements. You can achieve this by mentally rehearsing manoeuvres such as tacking and gybing so they become automatic. Imagine the sequence of events while racing, and study what is going to happen at each stage.

Practise-on-the-water procedures that you find difficult to imagine. Parts that seem unclear in your mind need more focus and practice. If they are unclear in your mind you will be hesitant when you perform them during a race.

Practice and preparation improve your confidence, and confidence leads to success.

For more information on the racing mind and body read *Mental and Physical Fitness for Sailing*, also published by Fernhurst Books.

CATAMARAN TACTICS

Tactics are manoeuvres carried out against another boat or boats. For an in-depth look at how to really mix it we recommend *Tactics* by Olympic Gold Medallist Rodney Pattisson, and *The Rules in Practice* by Bryan Willis, both published by Fernhurst Books.

When racing catamarans upwind you have fewer opportunities to dice than in a dinghy, because it takes longer to tack. However, a cat can gybe more quickly (and often more safely) than a dinghy flying a spinnaker, so duelling on the run is pretty important.

Basically, though, your objective is to blast round the course as fast as possible. Buoys become like roundabouts – think ahead which exit you want to take, and plan your entry accordingly.

In fact, because you're going so fast, you need to think 500 yards ahead all the time. Try not to be panicked into making a crash tack – you'll lose miles. Even worse is having to admit you're in the wrong and do penalty turns. You could lose a whole leg!

THE PRACTICE RACE

Use the practice race as a training exercise, not a race. Your objectives should be:
● Familiarisation with the committee boat and the way the committee run the race.
● Recognition of buoys.
● Familiarisation with the surroundings/coast/harbour and local conditions.
● To practise your pre-start sequence.
● To start.
● To sail one triangle.
● To check your boatspeed.
● To make adjustments, if necessary stopping and joining in the later stages of the race (and then retiring).
● To check the tidal flow: how strong is it? Which way does it go? Where is it stronger/weaker?

Having sailed the practice race, go home. Make any adjustments or alterations, then rest. Consider what you have learned, including the lessons of your mistakes. If you did well don't get over-confident. If you blew it don't get psyched out. Be positive.

Now – on with the regatta!

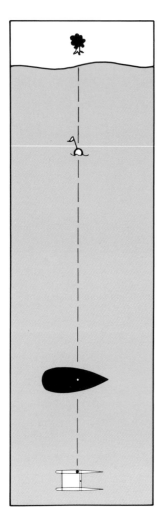

◆ Taking a transit: sail outside the line and sight along it to a fixed object.

PRE-START RESEARCH

Before going afloat obtain a chart of the area which will give you information about the depth of water you are sailing in and the tidal flow, paying particular attention to any back eddies. You should also know the times of high and low water.

Read the sailing instructions and understand clearly what they are telling you, together with the flags involved.

Before each start check the tidal flow by sailing up to a starting buoy or the committee boat. Look for the way the water sweeps by the buoy. If necessary, drop something (such as an orange) by the buoy and see how it drifts. If possible, check a static mark halfway up the beat for tidal flow. This will give you the direction of the tide and some idea which may be the best way up the first beat.

Next, sail to the outside of the start line and take a transit. These are especially useful if the line is long (as it must be in big fleet sailing). You can take a transit from anything static although larger, more prominent objects are preferable: when you are on the starting line you will need a transit that is clearly visible. It is very reassuring, particularly when making a mid-line start, to be able to move forward until your transit tells you you're just behind the line!

So now the ten-minute gun is imminent and your pulse is quickening. Remember: if you never achieve anything else at least start in front! Starting is a skill of its own. A good start does not rely on a correctly tuned boat or good boatspeed, but only the ability to be in the right place at the right time. There is only one way to get good at starts, and that is to practise them. Get in there and go for it. Sailors who are hesitant and avoid getting in among the action will never get good starts. Practise, take chances bit by bit and eventually you will get the brilliant start you've been dreaming of.

But why is a good start so important to your race? Think of it like this: the more boats you get ahead of at the start, the less you have to pass. It makes for slow sailing if you have to concentrate on passing other boats before you can think about the strategy of the race. So when you get a good start it not only gives you a psychological advantage, it gives you a strategic one too.

Your game plan for the start will vary as the championship or regatta progresses. Early in the event you will be keen to get some good results under your belt and you should be more willing to take chances. Later on, if your results look like being in the top ten you should start to sail more conservatively and more cautiously. But even so, you should know when to take chances and when to play safe.

We were sailing in a 300-boat championship and we had to get a result in the top 20 to win. It was the final race and as we took our run in to the start it looked bad. There were too many boats around us. In a split second, with a minute to the start, we gybed around and came in again with clear air, a gap to leeward and a brilliant start. We came off that line like a bullet. We achieved our result in the top 20. And won the championship.

So stay cool, be calm and confident. It pays off, and it wins championships!

AFTER THE TEN-MINUTE GUN

We always use a proven set pre-start sequence. We arrive early at the starting area and carry out our preliminary checks. When the ten-minute gun is fired we start a watch and check out the line to determine which end is favoured and where to start. This leaves us a couple of minutes to check the boat before the five-minute gun goes and the real fun begins.

There are several ways to check the start line. The first is to sail to windward across each end of the line. On one tack you may find you are pointing at a better angle towards the first mark: this is the end to start because it will reduce your distance up the first beat.

Another way to test the line is to sail to the middle of the line and point the boat head-to-wind with the jib flapping. Check whether the beams of the boat are pointing down the line; if not, judge which end of the line is favoured.

Try to be near the committee boat when the five-minute gun is fired. This is the most important signal and your timing must be accurate: the race starts five minutes after the five-minute gun (NOT ten minutes after the ten-minute gun).

Keep alert now. The start line will be congested and collisions happen when people are not paying attention. Be aware that the wind may swing to favour a particular end of the line and you may have to do a last-minute dash to the favoured end, so watch other boats that are still trying the line. Check their tacking angle to make sure you are planning to start in the right place.

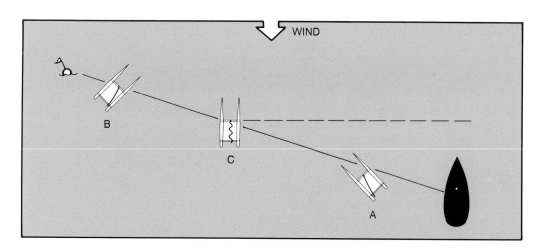

WIND

B

C

A

◆ Assessing the line: boat A can almost beat along the line, while B is crossing it at almost 90 degrees. So start – probably on starboard – at B's end. Sighting along the beams while heading directly upwind (C) will give the same conclusion.

With two to three minutes to go you should be making your final run into the starting area. Note how many boats have the same idea and don't let them affect your start. Either slow down or increase your speed to get to your ideal position.

Be flexible; don't barge in to start where you want to irrespective of the rules! Bargers at the start are unpleasant creatures and always sail into trouble eventually.

THE FINAL TWO MINUTES

- Line up with two to three minutes to go.
- Open up a gap to leeward by flapping the sails and luffing. This is vital: at the start you can then bear away and go for maximum speed.
- The crew keeps one jibsheet in each hand. Pull in the windward one if you want to brake. Dump it and pull in the leeward one if you want to go forwards.
- Don't allow boats to sail over the top of you: move forwards if you have to.
- Keep an eye on your watch.
- Make sure your crew is hooked onto the trapeze and ready to go.
- If you need to stop, steer sharply one way, then the other.
- Just before the starting gun, accelerate by sheeting in to the setting for maximum power, and by bearing away into the gap to leeward.

Now go, go, go for speed!

SQUARE LINE

On a square line start in the middle, aiming for plenty of room and clear air. You should be able to achieve this: the boats are normally more spread out on a square line.

To do this you must have a transit. That way you *know* when you're behind the line and can move forward confidently, even when your neighbours are hanging back. In fact, because of the way you sight 'through' the bow, most lines have a bulge back in the middle.

If you can't get a transit, perhaps because you're so far out to sea, beware of starting in the middle especially when the line is long and the 'round the ends' rule is in force. You must be sure you are not going to be over the line before the start, since you may not have time to sail around the ends before the gun.

If there is a bulge forwards, with many boats over, you must be in the bulge but with your sails alongside the other rigs. That's the best you can do. Don't risk pushing ahead of the bulge, especially if the black flag is flying, signifying sudden death if you're over. The black flag can not only ruin your whole day, it can wreck your regatta.

PORT-BIASED LINE

This is a difficult start for catamarans, especially in large fleets. Everyone wants to start at the port end, especially the top sailors. With a few minutes to go you will see boats negotiating their way down the line, jostling for position.

The idea is to start on starboard at the pin end of the line as the gun goes. Easier said than done! Careful judgement and accurate timing are essential. If you arrive too early and are pushed down the line you will not be able to cross the line and at best will have to bear off behind the line to gybe and try to re-start. Boats often become rafted up together head-to-wind. To avoid this and play the percentages, you should start two or three boat lengths from the pin end of the line. This enables you to miss the congestion on the starting mark, yet still get a reasonable start with minimal trouble by bearing away into a gap to get good boatspeed as the gun goes. Once you've got your nose ahead, tack to put yourselves in the lead.

It is often better to sail safe in large fleets and avoid port-tack starts. As a compromise you can start on starboard tack as close to the port end as possible. But if the line is very biased you may decide to have a go at a port-tack start. Be warned – you are living dangerously! Don't try it if you have poor boatspeed. You will never cross ahead of the fleet in time.

If you are fast, confident and racing in a small fleet with a line that allows plenty of room, it is worth attempting a port-tack start. You may be the lucky one. A port tack start is useful if you have nothing to lose. We once crossed a 200-boat fleet on port and survived but it really does need good communication between helmsman and crew. The helmsman should be concentrating on sailing the boat as fast as possible with the crew directing the operation, instructing him whether to 'duck' or 'dive' between boats. If you have low blood pressure, lots of bottle and are well insured, try it! If you are not an experienced sailor or are in doubt start on starboard tack at the port end.

STARBOARD-BIASED LINE

A starboard-biased line is going to give a congested start because everyone wants to start by the committee boat. This allows you very little margin for error.

If you do decide to go for the pole position, timing is everything. Aim to sail up to the committee boat (or limit

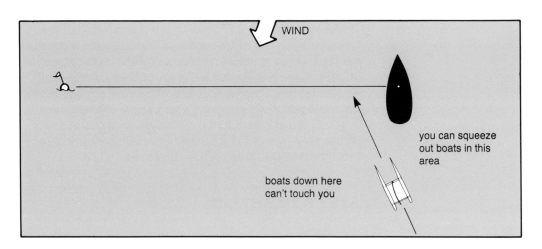

WIND

you can squeeze
out boats in this
area

boats down here
can't touch you

mark) as slowly as possible. Then the boats to leeward
can't push you out and the boats to windward will be
squeezed the wrong side of the committee boat.

If you come in too early **stop** by backing the jib and
steering violently. Try to avoid reaching down the line,
because the boats to leeward will push you over. If you
come in late you will find a wall of boats between you and
the wind. In this case keep high, because they sometimes
bear off too early, leaving a gap by the committee boat for
you to sail through.

Watch out for boats trying to reach in: they have no
rights, but they can ruin your start. Shout early to warn
them off, or luff over the line.

If you decide not to attempt pole position, start further
down the line with space and clear air. As usual, approach
slowly, creating space by steering hard to windward, then
to leeward.

If you get a bad start, look for space and then tack for
clear air. You won't lose much if you do this quickly, and
clip transoms all the way out to the right-hand side of the
course.

▲ Going for pole position on a
starboard-biased line.

GENERAL RECALLS

In large-fleet sailing general recalls are unfortunately
becoming the norm. They are a negative that needs to be
turned into a positive, so use them to your advantage.

Once you have sight of the recall flag carry on sailing for
a few minutes. Ask yourself how well you started. How
could it have been improved? How was your boatspeed?
What adjustments need to be made?

Once you have made a few mental notes, don't delay. Often you get only a five-minute gun for the next start, so get back down to the starting area. A keen race officer will aim to get the fleet away again quickly and you don't want to be dawdling up the beat while your opponents are back at the starting area lining up for the next start.

When you get back to the start line check that the race officer hasn't moved it. If he has, you will have to make a quick reassessment of your starting tactics.

AFTER THE START

We always try to keep our heads well down after the start. Once the boat is sailing at maximum speed, the crew should look around to see how things are going. Was the start a good or bad one? What's happening to other boats? Is the wind shifting? Have we got clear air? Should we tack off? Is there any information that the helmsman should know about?

Go for 100 per cent concentration and singlemindedness. Determine that, come what may, you are going to win this race. The crew should be sailing as low on the trapeze as possible with the jib set correctly. Sail fast to get clear air and take up a commanding position.

Think about what decisions you are going to have to make. Too often you see helmsmen and crews looking around thinking 'Wow, what a great start!' Don't be complacent; keep fighting. There's a long way to go yet.

Above all, keep an eye on the fleet. But don't deviate from your plan unless you are sure it's become the wrong thing to do. A good example cropped up in 1991 when we were sailing at the Dart World Championship with 300 boats on the start line. The legs of the course were over two miles long and it was impossible to see the windward mark. There had been many general recalls and we began to notice that the wind was swinging. The start line was over a mile long.

We had a good start and set off for the horizon. We arrived at the windward mark in first place, but with only half the fleet behind us. To leeward in the distance, some miles off, was the other half of the fleet going around the wing mark. To this day we can only assume they had not noticed the windshift and had become confused because of the size of the course. The race turned into a nightmare. Here we were in first place, ready to win the largest

World Championship ever held anywhere, any time, with boats going in all directions. It's at times like this you have to be sure your mind is not playing tricks on you. Was there a windshift? Should we go with the majority? We stuck to our plans, and we were right. We won the championship.

SHIFTS: TO TACK OR NOT?

Unlike monohulls catamarans take a long time to tack and tacking on every shift will probably lose you distance rather than gain it. Having said that, it is obviously an advantage to be skilful at tacking on shifts. Experience will tell you which windshifts are worth tacking on and which should be ignored. If you have a compass you can use it to confirm your hunches about the size of each shift.

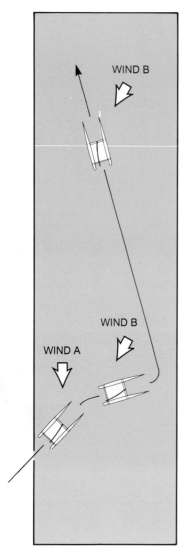

WIND B

WIND B

WIND A

◆ Don't tack on every shift, since you'll lose more than you gain – but if you get a big header, tack to take advantage of it.

When we get headed we normally give it time. Is the wind going to swing back again? If you're in a really bad header you should tack off, but try not to make rash decisions that may be disadvantageous. Be alert and look ahead at the rest of the fleet to see what is happening? Are they being headed? In short, only tack on major headers.

Look around at the sky and see what weather is coming in and whether it can be used to your advantage. We sometimes sail towards new weather if it looks favourable and we're desperate!

THE BEAT: FIRST TACK

In catamaran racing tacking should be kept to a minimum up the first beat. It may be best to make the mark in only two tacks. However, if you want to sail safely, especially up the first beat when you may not be sure which side of the course is favoured, it may be better to put in four tacks and keep to the middle of the course. By going up the middle you reduce the risk, and by the next beat you should have decided which side is favoured by monitoring the performance of other boats.

Unbelievably, we have noticed some sailors taking the wrong side of the course time after time, losing more and more places. Don't do it. This is not a rehearsal, so give it your best. CLEAR YOUR MIND. THINK!

You may have to tack off sooner than anticipated if you are in dirty wind. It is better to put in a couple of extra tacks for clear air than be slowed down by sailing in someone else's dirt.

Remember not to oversheet when you come out of a tack. Power up your sails, and only sheet in to the normal position as your speed increases.

FIRST BEAT – SECOND TACK

Ideally your second tack should be on the layline to the mark. If you are some way off, a crew with a good eye is a great asset when deciding whether you can make the windward mark or not.

Of course, the best way to approach the windward mark is in the lead! You can then sail your own course. Everyone else will have to modify his ideal approach, and the further down the fleet you are the greater the compromise will be.

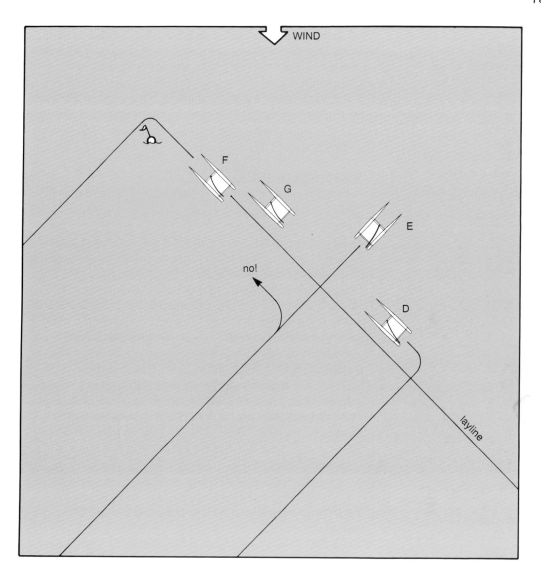

Aim to approach on starboard tack so you have right of way. You do not have to give room to boats coming in on port.

Tacking onto the layline late is fine if you have a commanding position. If not, and you come in on port close to the buoy, you will have the problem of dirty, confused air and you will have to sail through the starboard boats before you can pick your space to tack for the layline. Avoid tacking beneath the starboard boats unless you are confident that they have overstood the mark sufficiently for you to get clear air as you sail to the mark.

◄ Boat D makes a good approach to the windward mark, tacking just over the layline to be safe. E needs to blast through the line of starboard boats before tacking, and should on no account tack to leeward of F or G.

As you approach the mark note what happened to the boats that went the opposite side of the beat to you and make a decision about which side of the beat you want to go next time.

If you are not sure about the tide have a look at the buoy as you pass. If the tide is pushing you onto the buoy, give it an extra-wide berth: don't risk hitting it at this early stage of the race.

Meeting other boats

Top sailors rarely seem to get into collisions and this is not because they are lucky. They actively aim to keep out of trouble by avoiding confrontations on the water. It has certainly been our philosophy to keep our noses clean and get on with the race with the minimum of aggravation, since such complications only slow you down.

If another boat is catching you up and sailing faster than you are, there is no point in hindering his progress. He will pass you in the end. You will learn more by letting him pass you and emulating the way he sails than by getting into a duel. It will slow you both down and there is always a pack of wolves ready for the kill coming up from behind.

The crew must be alert at all times to other boats on the course who may have right of way over you. A good crew can judge another boat's speed and save you a sudden tack or a desperate duck. The stronger the breeze the faster your boatspeed, so the earlier you will need to take avoiding action.

If you do need to bear away behind a boat on starboard, it's better to ease sheets and slow down. If you simply bear away your speed will increase and the problem gets worse.

At all costs avoid a collision. It is better to argue who was in the right afterwards in front of a Protest Committee than risk a collision that could put you out of the whole series. It's hard to win when your hull is reduced to matchwood!

ROUNDING THE WINDWARD MARK

Places can be gained at the windward mark by smart thinking and a good buoy rounding.

As you approach, remember the tide – if it's pushing you onto the buoy you'll need to allow more room than if the current is helping you.

Next, have a good look at the competition: it's usually pretty crowded around the mark, particularly at the end of the first beat. In a large fleet it is always better to approach the windward mark on starboard tack. But be sure that when you tack to lay the mark you have clear air and that you can reach the mark without having to point up too much: our advice is to deliberately overstep the mark a bit. If you tack underneath other boats they will inevitably sail over the top of you, your air will be disturbed, you will point lower and go slower and may even have to make another tack to get clear air. Disaster! No, be confident and sail just that bit further before you tack for the mark, and take a commanding position.

If you have come up the left-hand side of the beat and are approaching the windward mark on port, you will be living dangerously – especially if you are not in the top few boats. Watch for a gap long before you reach the mark or layline. Plan your path to the layline, deciding which boats you're going to cross (pass ahead of) and which boats you're going to duck (go behind).

Look ahead and see what is happening to the other boats. Are they making the mark? If they are struggling or having to put in an extra tack, think ahead, sail on and tack further ahead. You must come into the mark with clear air.

THE FIRST REACH

Steer *gently* around the windward mark onto the reach, easing the main and jibsheets. Simultaneously, the crew should move back and reach for the restraining line. Get ready to enjoy the ride!

Being first on the reach can gain you an enormous advantage because you can sail the shortest, most direct course to the next mark. Everyone else has to defend his wind.

The first reach on a catamaran course is usually a close reach and in our experience it rarely pays to go low: stay high, aim for clear wind at all times and blast over the top of them. If, however, the wind is dropping it may pay to go low and head up to the mark later, increasing the apparent wind when you need it. It nearly always pays to go low if the tide is pushing you to weather: most people will go high and will have to run back down to the mark against the tide. That's slow!

To protect your wind on a reach, give a little luff to indicate to those behind that you mean business.

The helmsman should be hiking hard with the crew concentrating on constantly trimming the jib. Keep

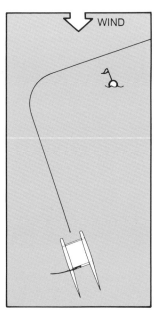

WIND

driving, powering up the sails but easing off as the hulls begin to nosedive. Keep your eye on the telltales and make maximum use of the gusts.

Think ahead: what is your plan for the next leg? Are you going to stand on past the mark or gybe on the mark? What implications does that have for the boats around you?

THE GYBE MARK

At the gybe mark you want to aim for the inside berth, calling for water if necessary. If you gybe on the mark you will have the advantage of clear wind on the next leg.

If you are towards the back of the fleet it's not easy to round close to the buoy. Look ahead and see if the boats in front are going to make the leeward mark. If not, you can gain advantage by sailing beyond the mark before gybing (see left).

THE SECOND REACH

The second reach is always broader than the first. As you round the gybe mark either luff so you can blast through to windward of the boats ahead, or continue on starboard for a while, gybe late and zoom through their lees. Which you choose depends on how the boats ahead are behaving. If they are luffing hard, go for the late gybe. If they are sailing straight for the leeward mark, gybe quickly and go through to weather. Of course, if you're ahead, or there aren't many boats around, go straight for the next mark.

ROUNDING THE LEEWARD MARK

Once you have rounded the wing mark you must be thinking ahead: your aim is to achieve the inside position at the leeward mark. It is important to get this right because you want to start the beat in a dominant position.

So look ahead as you approach the mark. Will you get the inside turn? Is the mark too congested? Is there anywhere for you to go? If you're not going to get the rounding you have planned, slow down and keep clear of the congestion – just let them go. Remember, you want the best position as you set out on the beat. So it is better to slow down now and get the inside turn; if you cruise around the outside you will just fade away once you start beating.

Having made some space, make a wide turn as you approach the mark but get tight to the buoy as you go around. This will ensure you're up there to windward on the beat and will leave your tacking options open.

NEXT BEAT

On the previous beat you should have noted whether the port or starboard side of the course is favoured. This is your chance to go the right way up the beat, having perhaps sailed conservatively up the first beat.

If there is a procession of boats behind you head high, forcing them to bear away and fall away to leeward. Once they are no longer a threat, bear away and sail a faster course.

◤ Boat H has done well to get above the line of boats, but J has no option but to bear away and try to get through K. Boat I doesn't have much option until someone tacks.

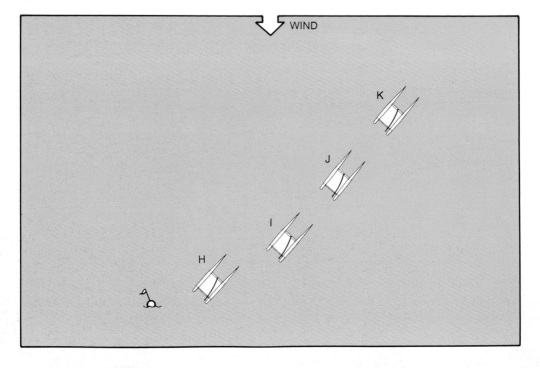

If you are unlucky and the boat ahead of you on the beat is sailing high and slow to defend his position, bear away and sail fast and free to leeward with the aim of trying to blast through his lee. If you still cannot pass him you have little alternative but to tack off for clear air.

At all costs aim for clear air and avoid the procession of boats sailing away from the mark. Aim to sail for speed for a couple of minutes and then assess the situation; if it is not looking good, tack off.

THE RUN

If you are a good helmsman but have had a setback in the early part of the race now is a good time to pass the slower sailors. Fast downwind sailing is a coveted art.

The best tactical advice is to sail your own race. Boatspeed is everything on the downwind leg and tactics are of secondary importance. So avoid getting into luffing duels. However, remember that the windward boat's windshadow extends *abeam* on the run (in the direction of the bridle telltale) so stay out of that if you're to leeward of someone. Get clear air, then sail fast and sail low!

How low you can point is a function of weight: the lighter you are the more you can bear away.

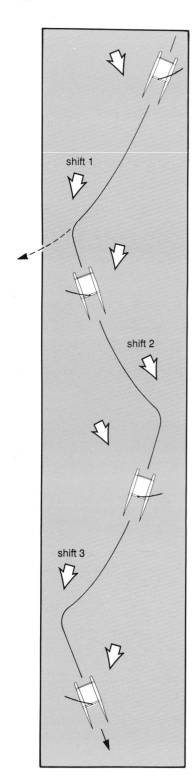

shift 1

shift 2

shift 3

Head up in the lulls and bear away in the gusts for maximum speed. If necessary, keep gybing to stay in a gust.

As you go down the run you should be thinking ahead. Where are we going on the next beat?

When to gybe on the run

• When the wind shifts: take the gybe that gives you the closest course to the mark.
• When you're getting anywhere near the layline: avoid the layline at all costs (just as you would avoid it on a beat. Indeed, the run is just like the beat in reverse).
• When you're running to the mark. It's better to put in an extra gybe or two than risk losing boatspeed so near the mark. You'll get overlapped, and overtaken.
• When you want to get an overlap on another boat.

AT THE LEEWARD MARK

If you have an overlap approaching a mark then you have the right to round inside the other boat. The rules state that the critical moment for judging the overlap is when the outside boat's bow is two lengths from the buoy. In a catamaran doing 20 knots this is slightly late, so start negotiating at five lengths.

◀ If the wind shifts, take the gybe that leads you most directly to the mark. Gybing is quick, so don't hesitate!

◆ Boat L has her overlap in time.

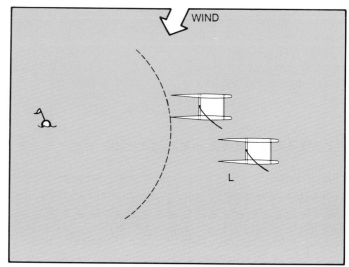

WIND

L

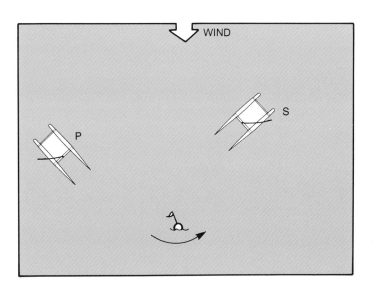

◀ As boat S is on starboard and also has an overlap she clearly has right of way.

The main problem at the leeward mark is boats converging on opposite gybes. In the diagram boat S clearly has right of way: she is on starboard *and* has an overlap. Boat P can either slow down by bearing away, waggling the rudder blades and moving weight aft, or gybe twice.

THE LAST BEAT

As the race develops the boats may become more spread out and the majority of placings will now be set within a few boats of each other. If you are not under threat from behind it may pay you to split tacks up the last beat with your opponent.

Note the changing conditions and use these to your advantage. A first place can sometimes be recovered when your opponent, hellbent on winning, does not notice what's going on and ignores windshifts, changes of tide, etc.

COVERING AND ATTACKING

In the early part of the race your efforts should be concentrated on taking the most advantageous course at the fastest possible speed. Up the last beat, however, it is worth covering the boat behind if he is posing a threat. To cover, you tack so that after regaining speed you are sitting on your opponent's apparent wind (the wind shown

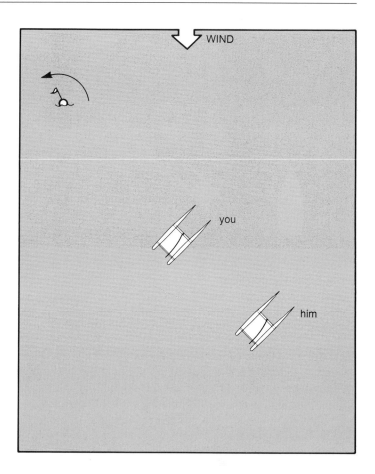

♦ Always stay between your opponent and the next mark, even if you're not covering.

by your wind indicator). This is quite difficult in a catamaran, because you lose 50–100 yards on tacking.

To avoid cover, simply wait for your opponent to tack on you, then tack yourself. He can't do two quick tacks in succession, so you'll escape. Alternatively, if he doesn't really get on your wind, ease both sheets two inches and power through his lee.

If you are in front, always keep between the boat behind and the next mark or finishing line. There is nothing more frustrating than losing a first place by becoming complacent up the last beat. If the boat behind does not pose a threat, keep your head down and sail fast: the race is not over yet!

If you are in the attacking position and your opponent has tacked for the finish line, provided there is no threat from behind, stand on a little. You may still gain an advantage if he makes a mistake or if the wind shifts or dies and you can sail more freely and directly to the finish line.

PART THREE

PREPARING
THE BOAT

◆ Check the hull alignment by measuring between the centre of each stern and from bow to bow: they should be the same. If they are not, you will have to file or fill the packing of the beams. Note that when the rig tension comes on the bows will 'toe in', but this is good news since it enables you to point higher.

Your boat needs to be set up properly onshore before you attempt any racing. You must then get into a routine of checking all the fittings each day at a regatta: that's the only way to guarantee trouble-free racing.

Firstly, check the hull alignment. The hulls must be parallel. The beams should be a good, tight fit in their housings and the securing bolts should make a snug fit. Lift one bow of the boat and check the deflection from bow to bow. The ultimate is to have no flexibility or 'paddle' between the hulls.

Attach the rudders and check that they are upright and also that they line up parallel with the centrelines of the hulls. Is each rudder tight in its stock? There should be no movement or twist.

◆ Check that the rudders are vertical. If not, adjust the pintles.

◆ Measure between the rudder trailing edges, then between the leading edges. The measurements should be the same. If not, adjust the tiller connecting bar (see opposite page).

If you have centreboards check these for alignment and for stiffness in their cases. They should be a good, tight fit with no sloppiness. If gaskets are allowed it is essential that they are well maintained so you get a smooth flow of water across the bottom of the boat.

Ensure that your rudder blades and centreboards are in line, and check that they aren't twisted since this can cause weather or lee helm.

Trampolines are attached in a variety of ways but you should always make sure you sail your boat with the trampoline pulled as tight as possible, so that in choppy conditions the trampoline does not hit the tops of the waves and you won't gravitate to the centre all the time when you're moving about the boat.

◄ Test for flexibility between the hulls by lifting one bow and checking that the other does not move (left). If it does move you will need to glass the beam sockets to make the beams a tight fit (top). On the Dart, make sure the beam clips are in place or the rig tension will pull the hulls out of alignment.

◄ The tiller bar on the Hobie 16 is telescopic, with a locking screw.

◄ The tiller bar on the Tornado can be adjusted by screwing the end in or out.

◄ On the Dart you have to take out the pop rivet and move the end fitting.

◆ Centreboard gaskets must be changed regularly. Stick each edge down with epoxy and fair them off with fibreglass filler.

Make sure the toestraps are sufficiently tight. Slack toestraps make hiking difficult and even more uncomfortable.

Regularly check all shackles and fittings to ensure they are working efficiently. Pay particular attention to the shackles at the top of the mast. Tape up shackles and split-pins wherever possible.

A little regular maintenance is more beneficial than a major annual overhaul. Boat maintenance should be a routine operation, not a chore! There are many ways of losing races which you cannot control, but this is one you can!

◆ Adjust the toestraps so you can get a fist beneath them. This gives a good compromise between the ideal tensions for beating and running.

◆ Tighten the nuts on the rudder assembly, packing them if necessary.

◆ The Hobie downhaul cleat will slip unless you file a slot in the mast for it.

PART FOUR

TUNING THE RIG

Always assess the conditions before going afloat so you have some idea whether you are setting your boat up for light, medium or strong winds. It is easier to alter the rig afloat on some catamarans than others; in particular the mast can be raked further aft quite easily on a Tornado, but this would be a dangerous manoeuvre on a Dart. So on a Dart you'll need to look ahead and guess the wind strength for the day, and maybe adopt a compromise setting. There is no doubt that if you are to be successful you must learn how to tune your boat. You cannot simply put the mast up and hope for the best.

MAST RAKE

Before putting up your mast check the shroud lengths – they can vary and mistakes are sometimes made by the manufacturer. Wire rigging will stretch so it pays to check the lengths from time to time anyway, especially if you have been sailing in strong winds.

Mast rake is critical. As a general rule in light winds the mast needs to be in a fairly upright position to increase power. As the wind increases more mast rake can be introduced. This enables you to point slightly higher and reduces weather helm. Save the maximum rake (aft) for strong winds.

Remember too that the lighter the combined crew weight the more mast rake you will need. The heavier the combined crew weight, the less rake you will need.

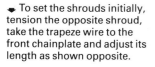

To set the shrouds initially, tension the opposite shroud, take the trapeze wire to the front chainplate and adjust its length as shown opposite.

Measuring mast rake

You need some initial settings to get you started and the best way to find them is to ask your sailmaker, a manufacturer or someone of your weight who is going fast. You can refine these settings in the light of experience.

It follows that you need to know how to measure mast rake. The method we suggest is using the trapeze wire as a measuring pendulum, as follows:

1 Disconnect the trapeze wire from the shockcord.

2 Make it as long as possible.

3 Rotate the mast: for example, if you have disconnected the port trapeze wire rotate the mast until the spanner is in line with the main beam on the starboard side. Lock the mast in this position by inserting the pin at the base.

4 Tension the rig by getting your partner to pull on the opposite shroud.

5 Swing the trapeze wire forward until it just touches the deck where the rear edge of the bridle chainplate crosses the deck. (If the trapeze wire isn't long enough, tie a suitable length of string to it, or hook on the luff downhaul from the mainsail.)

6 Put a marker at this position on the trapeze wire. Keeping it stretched, move aft until the marked position touches the edge of the deck. This new position (the 'datum point') gives a measure of mast rake.

7 Measure from the spot you have found to the transom.

On a Dart, if the spot is between the centre toe loop and the rear beam then you may assume there is no aft rake on the mast.

◆ The Tornado has an adjustable forestay fitting to control mast rake.

◆ Set the length of the trapeze until the bottom of the metal fitting just touches the chainplate (left). Then take the wire to the gunwale near the stern and make a mark where it touches (centre). The distance from this mark to the stern is a measure of mast rake (right).

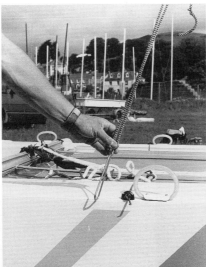

Basically, as the wind increases more mast rake is required to de-power the rig. This has the effect of moving the centre of effort aft thereby reducing power. Increasing the mast rake also opens the leech, and the boat becomes more manageable without loss of performance.

DIAMOND WIRES

Tight diamonds bend the mast so the middle of the mast bows forwards, away from the mainsail. This takes out the curve built into the luff of the sail, reducing fullness in the main. If your boat is rigged with diamonds you can set them up to suit the wind strength.

In light winds tension the diamonds to bend the mast and reduce the fullness of the sail.

In medium winds slacken the diamonds, straighten the mast and increase the fullness in the main.

In strong winds flatten the main again by increasing diamond tension. This also makes the downhaul more effective.

◆ Tensioning the diamonds bends the mast and flattens the sail (left). On the Tornado the tension is adjusted by a bottle screw at the foot of the mast (right).

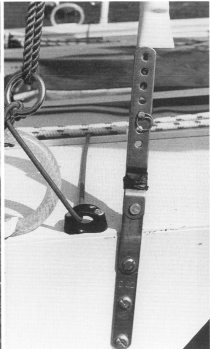

↤ This is our light to medium wind forestay setting on the Dart. In strong winds we lengthen it by an inch and a half.

↤ This is the chainplate setting for light to medium winds. In strong winds the pin goes down to the bottom hole.

↤ These settings give good rig tension while allowing the mast to rotate easily – using finger pressure only.

RIG TENSION

One way of measuring rig tension is by pushing one of the chainplate adjusters forwards, hard, and measuring the distance vertically from the deck to the uppermost point on the clevis pin hole. With a slack rig, the chainplate will swing quite a lot, and the vertical distance will be small. Remember the general rule: the stronger the breeze, the more rig tension you should use.

Obviously forestay length, shroud length, mast rake and mast tension are all inter-related. The simplest way to think of it is that the forestay length determines the mast rake, then the shrouds determine the rig tension. The shrouds pull back against the forestay: tightening the shrouds pulls back more, this is resisted by the forestay, and all three wires just get tighter.

When you have got the rig the way you want it for one set of conditions, we suggest you record the forestay length, the mast rake 'datum point', and the rig tension.

← On the Tornado the rig tension is resisted by a dolphin stay (the Hobie has a wire version).

BATTENS

Different types of battens have different bend characteristics. If you sail a strict one-design catamaran then you have an easier life, because the batten design has already been decided for you. However, if the sail choice is yours, then you also have to decide on which battens to use.

Generally a certain cut of mainsail will need a certain type of batten. It is always advisable to research sail and batten compatibility. Both are expensive, and by trial and error you will end up with lots of different permutations of both. If you are not sure, ask around in your class and decide on a mast/sail/batten/ combination that is proven. However, you may find that your chosen combination doesn't suit you and you will want to try others. Such is life.

You will also need to consider the wind strength. Different wind strengths need different battens, so if the rules allow, use stiffer battens in stronger winds to flatten the sail, particularly near the head. Also, lighter crews will need stiffer battens.

← To tension the battens correctly, simply push them in and tie them so the material is pulled up tight – and no more.

Batten tension

Although sails are cut to a set fullness an advantage can be gained in medium airs by increasing the tension on the battens. This has the effect of increasing fullness in the sail and making the sail more powerful.

Conversely in a strong breeze the top battens can be loosened in their pockets to flatten the sail. Class rules permitting, stiffer battens can be used to flatten the sail and gain an advantage. In a strict one-design class, when you cannot change battens, you may be able to turn the top battens end-to-end to increase stiffness at the luff.

Whatever you do, make sure you tie in the battens securely and that the tension is equal on each batten.